CHURCH
LEADERSHIP

Ray Evans

Copyright © 2016 by Ray Evans

First published in Great Britain in 2016

British Library Cataloguing in Publication Data
A record for this book is available from the British Library

ISBN: 978-1-910587-74-4

Designed by Diane Warnes
Printed in Denmark by Nørhaven

10Publishing, a division of 10ofthose.com
Unit C, Tomlinson Road, Leyland, PR25 2DY, England
Email: info@10ofthose.com
Website: www.10ofthose.com

CONTENTS

SERIES INTRODUCTION

The Hub Conference was launched in 2013 by the Fellowship of Independent Evangelical Churches (FIEC) as an annual conference to help men and women find clear routes into independent church ministry. For those 'just looking' as well as those 'just started', The Hub aims to be one means of support and advice on a possible journey through training and into gospel ministry.

Led by experienced gospel workers from the FIEC, and supported by leaders from colleges and courses, The Hub provides Bible ministry and a wide range of seminars on ministry-related issues.

It is out of this annual conference that this series of books was born. It occurred to the organising committee that these seminar topics could provide a helpful resource for anyone involved in gospel ministry, whether or not they attended The Hub or entered paid Christian ministry. In addition, the hope is that these books might also help pastors and leaders in discipling members of congregations for leadership and ministry.

Someone once described theological books as a *'college of teachers committed to helping you do your best to handle the Word of truth'*. We hope this series will play a small but significant part in that library of wisdom, at whatever stage you find yourself.

Leadership, or often a lack of it, is one of the greatest challenges facing the local church today. As a leader of a growing church with decades of experience, Ray Evans has thought long and hard on the subject. His distilled wisdom, obvious expertise and long experience are condensed into this latest title in our `Ministry Journeys` series. It is written in a very accessible style for anyone involved in leadership in the local church – not only pastors and elders but also those who have responsibility for leading any ministry team in a church.

Trevor Archer and Dan Green
Series editors

INTRODUCTION

We hear the word leadership a lot, but what exactly does it mean? Derek Prime, an experienced Christian leader quotes this definition, '[Leadership is] the ability to encourage and equip other leaders.'[1] That seems like an enormous task, doesn't it? Not one to be taken on lightly... if at all. But what if you feel God is calling you into that very position?

If that is so, we will soon find ourselves faced with a myriad of questions.

'How can I be a leader? How can I lead others – God's people... even God's leaders! I don't think so... I'm not even sure how I'd start to work that out, even if God wanted me to do it! I'm not up to it. I can't do it... maybe God will call someone else.'

If that sounds like you, you're in good company. Moses, that great leader of God's people, couldn't quite get his head around what he was being asked to do when God called him into leadership of his people, Israel. God's call was on his life, but Moses balked at the whole idea. Frankly, he didn't feel equal to the task (see Ex. 3 and 4).

Of course, with hindsight, we can see that it was obvious that the Lord had been preparing him for the job he was calling him to do; God always equips us when he asks us to step up or step out. A spell at the top of the ancient Egyptian world, hard knocks in the school of life – where Moses faced misunderstanding and personal rejection – and the difficult years of managing the unruly on a daily basis (even if it was a flock of sheep!) had all been part of God's wonderful preparation of this great servant-leader. It is worth checking out C.S. Lewis's great insights into those 'long, monotonous years of adversity'.[2]

As you may be pondering the question, 'Does the Lord want me involved in leading his people in some way?', you too may also be questioning whether you are 'fit for purpose'.

One part of answering that question is to recognise that the Lord has been moulding you into the person he wants you to be – and that he has been doing that all your life.[3] Like Moses, many of us can't see what the Lord is or has been accomplishing in us, and others can. We need encouragement to reflect on all that God has been doing and preparing us for.

Professor Donald Macleod, former principal of the Free Church College, Edinburgh, was once asked about the need for an assured 'call' to the ministry before taking a change of life direction. I heard his response and it surprised me. He said that in his own experience, and his colleagues' opinion, those with a very strong sense of 'call' were often the least capable, and those with a very questioning and even unsure sense, were those with greater ability. Those with a *willingness to serve*, as their church requested them, had gone on to be a blessing to the cause of Christ.[4] So if you don't feel up to the job, or are questioning whether God is asking this of you at all, don't let that put you off exploring what the Lord may have for you in terms of leadership.

I certainly couldn't see in myself 'leadership qualities' before I got involved in serving his people. I started in (very) small ways, but as others encouraged me, and with my willingness to serve, it led to training and then taking on the responsibility of being a pastor of a church. I had only the vaguest sense that I had 'leadership capability'. But looking back – as you may do too – it is possible to see that the various experiences the Lord allows can all be used by him to make a potential leader for his people.

LIFE AND LEADERSHIP

So let's look a little more closely at what that might mean.

For me, on reflection, being in the Scouts was formative. I lived on a small RAF camp as a boy. The Scout troop consisted of just 10 boys (at one time there were only three of us). There were two patrols, each headed by a patrol leader and an assistant, leaving three others per patrol. With my friend John, I had been there the longest, and now that we had a few more boys we could form a 'proper' troop; so he and I became PLs by default. Before I even realised I was in a place of leadership, and before the phrase 'sweat the small stuff' was invented, I had to make sure the patrol came up to scratch every week.[5] Did everyone have clean hands and fingernails? (Do you know how hard that is to achieve with five boys aged 11 to 14?) Did everyone have a pencil and notebook? Was everyone's woggle straight? I used to worry about getting it right, as there was fierce but friendly competition between the two patrols for coveted points. At the time it seemed painfully unnecessary – why couldn't we just get on with Scoutcraft, games and sports – yet the repetition of patrol inspection week after week formed in me a habit that became useful in the week-by-week demands of Christian ministry.

Maybe you can see something in your own life that has similarly helped you.

The '1st Headley (Headley Court)' troop also taught me about 'awkward man' management. Full of characters whom I can clearly see in my mind's eye, here was no conformist, obedient and submissive workforce who would do as they were told because they wanted a bonus at the end of the year, or didn't want to get fired! Unbeknownst to me I was learning to motivate, guide and unify a group of people who were all 'volunteers'. 'Hiring and firing' doesn't come into play in a Scout troop. If they don't like it – or you – they will leave. A lot like church, really. So here was a key skill being developed without me being aware of it. People skills that are so necessary for leading a church often don't just 'appear' when we are converted to Christ, but have been moulded by real-life experiences over many years, and from a young age, and are then sanctified by the Holy Spirit. What 'people skills' may have already been ingrained in you through your life's experiences?

SCHOOL

School was another formative time. What are your memories? Far too many to retell or write down, no doubt. But some may stand out. Let me tell you of just one of mine. For me, learning the discipline of revising for and taking tests – it seemed like *all the time* – was a bugbear. I must have taken thousands of them from a young age until my last public exam when I was in my early 20s. Being a classic first-born – anxious, introverted, shy, conformist, easily embarrassed, conscientious and feeling out of my depth much of the time – I used to study hard for tests (wanting to avoid a telling-off more than any need to succeed or prove myself). Of course there were many times as I got older when I questioned, 'What's the point of all this?' and 'Why do I have to go through so much nervous anxiety and emotional pain to do these? Isn't there an easier way?' But at school you just have to keep ploughing on as the tests get more serious in consequence. Years later, and a well-trained memory as a result, I and the church I serve have reaped huge benefits from what I misjudged as all those fruitless hours.

Now, 'school' for you may not have been like that. But there will be lessons God can use to better equip you. What was it about a great teacher you admired? Their discipline in class, their high expectations of everyone, their diligence in marking your work, their humanity and sense of fun as term came to an end? What put you off poor teachers? Their selfishness and basic unfairness in the way they treated people? Their sarcastic demeanour? Their arbitrary put-downs and the way they generated fear through nasty threats? Their laziness? Would-be church leader, emulate the former, flee from the latter.

It may have been 'playground rules' that shaped you. Most children probably realise before they are five that some people are bullies and you need to learn how to deal with them. How to befriend new kids, how to share things, how to let others have their way, but also being able to say what you want – these are lessons to learn that are all relevant in church leadership. For me, school dinner-time was often difficult. I was always 'vertically challenged', being the second shortest boy in my year for the whole of school life, right up until I grew a few inches and reached the dizzy height of five feet eight (and a half) when I was in the Sixth Form. So around the dinner table I was an easy one to overlook – especially when I was only in the third form (Year 9) and on my assigned table there were two Lower Sixth 'men' (Year 12) who had enormous appetites, hairy faces, and who enjoyed intimidating me. Every day was a learning curve! It helped me understand and feel what 'an underdog' has to go through. Too often 'successful' church leaders can come across as 'having it all together' with little emotional intelligence towards those who struggle with life. But even school dinner-time can be used to make you a more empathetic person.

Reflect for a few moments about your main memories of school, and ponder how they may be used to advantage by the Lord to make you a better leader of others.

FURTHER EDUCATION

Many have the privilege of going to university or college. What did you learn there? (A question many ask as their tuition fees rack up!) Two lessons stand out for me – relative loneliness, and anxiety about the unknown. That sounds weird when it is meant to be the time when you make good friends and have a great time. Well, I did both, but underlying it all, those emotions and thoughts stand out.

The first was because of the realisation that no one was going to do any of it for you. Just getting out of bed and to lectures was entirely your own responsibility. If you didn't turn up, no one was going to come looking. One day I was really ill, and I was struck by how isolating uni can be – I didn't see a soul all day long as I kept being sick in my room. But what all this meant was that the 'self-starter' mechanism was being deepened within. And that is a key quality in Christian ministry. So much of leadership is about being 'alone'; not so much because you are 'aloof at the top', but because a great deal of the preparation is done in lonely study time. If you can't self-start, it will only be seen much later on – after heartache for you and the church. All those essay deadlines, seminars scheduled just when a great match was on TV, choices to make about whether to get the work done and delay the gratification until after (or the other disastrous way round) all help mould character.

And character is what gets tested in ministry all the time – and in numerous small ways.

What felt a complete hassle at the time was preparation for the future. As a minister, you can't easily say, 'I'm really busy. Can we put Sunday back a couple of days until I am prepared?' It's an immovable feast, and your job is often to serve the meal – on time – every week. Have you learned that self-discipline yet? (Don't be tempted to whine. Think about how much 'self-starting' a mum of three hungry children has to have, as meal times come round for her family about every four hours, every part of the waking day, every week!)

What about anxiety at uni? Ever felt it? I did, right from the beginning. Everyone else seemed so mature – in my first few days, I thought most of the people I saw must surely be in their final year. They seemed so über-confident, so clever, so at ease compared to me. Anxiety didn't easily go away as new worries piled in – the first essay being roundly critiqued, and then, all too quickly, the first set of exams – 'Preliminary to Part One of the Geography Tripos' – didn't feel very preliminary to me; and then the first 'proper' girlfriend (who became my wife!).

Anxiety can be a negative and destructive thing. We are told to cast all our care upon him, for he cares for us (1 Pet. 5:7). But there is a 'concern for all the churches' (2 Cor. 11:28, NKJV) that is right and proper.

That was far more onerous than the physical pain of toil and trouble Paul lists. Where did he develop an instinct for dealing with a harmful anxiety (Phil. 4:6) while keeping the proper concern which leads to a caring, pastoral approach (e.g. 2 Cor. 11:2 –3; 1 Thes. 2:6–12)? I picked up a lot on how to handle anxiety at uni. I learned to distinguish between the things that matter and those which really don't; and the things you must do something about, and those which you can't control. Exam fear would hit, many a person would go into a tailspin, be paralysed by nerves, and then would perform badly. Some hardly revised (one such guy started sobbing uncontrollably in a second-year exam), and some so over-revised that they just couldn't do the exam well. I realised that I had absolutely no control over what questions would be asked, but I did need to prepare well by revising and practising hard. Every question in my syllabus required a one-hour essay – three per exam for every exam of each year. It was hard (the second-year exam timetable was a three-hour exam Thursday afternoon, two three-hour exams on Friday, one on Saturday morning, two on Monday and one on Tuesday). Later in life I would have to prepare 30 minute talk after 30 minute talk and try to develop that same internal clock mechanism which knows when time is up and when to stop (my church would say that I was more successful at uni!). But what a training ground.

Anxiety has also been a blessing when it comes to people awareness. Looking out for the 'needy, new and neglected' is a pastoral staple. You always have to be concerned for 'sheep on the fringe'. A healthy, internalised, tacit sense in church life of 'Successes, Weaknesses, Threats and Opportunities' (a ready-to-use SWOT analysis) can result from a concern for others. Again I wasn't consciously aware that God was developing all this in me while I was growing up into a man (as per Kipling's poem, and the seeing through those imposters of success and failure).[6] What about you through your time at college or uni? It may be very different indeed from my experience, but that is because God is shaping you for what he wants for your life – and no two are clones. So what do you think he may have already done to prepare you for leadership?

JOBS AND CAREER

You may still be at uni, or you may have gone straight into work and by now be in your first or second job, and in the early years of a career. What are you making of it? Have you seen the leadership lessons God is teaching you? Or are you assuming that 'nothing like that is happening'? God doesn't waste anything in forming you to be like Christ and making you useful to his work (See Philemon 11 and the play on words around Onesimus' name – he who was formerly 'Useless' is now 'Useful').

Most of us work for someone, so already you may have seen how key the boss is to everyone's well-being. It is reckoned that 80 per cent of people don't leave a job when they move on – they leave a boss! Now that is a key lesson. Humanly speaking the quality of leadership in a church is a KPI – Key Performance Indicator, to use jargon from work.[7]

Look at the diagram below.

Where would you put your present boss? What about your present pastor (ouch!)? What about yourself?

Two Vital Leadership Competencies

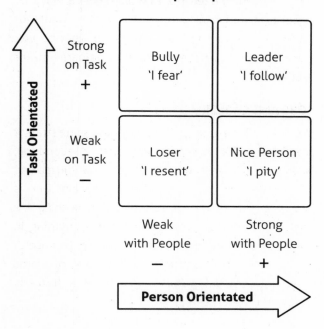

You may have already sensed that good leadership is a combination of competency in two areas – good at helping people, and good at getting (often repetitive) tasks done. Reflect on how this is seen in your present job, and think about how this can go well – or badly – at church. You can see how a business, or service provision, can be marred by a serious weakness in either zone – the church is no different. Ask God to help you grow in whatever area you need to strengthen so that you won't be a liability, but an asset, to whatever you may lead in the future.

What other leadership lessons is your job teaching you, which God can use to bless his people through you in the future? For me, an enduring one came in a strange way. For a while I was a window cleaner. It would take too long to explain why, with two Cambridge degrees, I was doing that, but there I was, roughly dressed, carrying a heavy wooden 21-foot extension ladder, armed with the all-important 'scrim' (the best cloth for cleaning windows). My 'real identity' – Christian – was hidden, as was my educational background. One person I worked for was a fairly famous author of Christian books. I don't want to sound harsh or judgemental, but I felt a bit 'looked down on' by the body language directed towards me. It didn't enamour me to the customer. What if I hadn't been a believer and had known who the person was? Could that have damaged the cause of Christ? How many times must I have done far worse?

I realised how easy it is to falsely judge others; and how important it is to treat everyone with great dignity, for all are made in the image of God (also see Heb. 13:2). If you work in an office, you may have already appreciated this factor. You will know who is a key person in the organisation – the person who greets at the reception desk. They set the tone for *everything else* that happens for visitors and new people. A good company or organisation will know that it is very hard to change that first impression. It is a lesson well worth learning for church leadership too.

There will be many lessons from the world of work. Don't see work as a 'waste' before a proper 'calling' to ministry which is paid for by other Christians. *We are all* FTCW (Full-Time Christian Workers, to use the LICC's helpful parlance), and the training and preparation for whatever avenue of service God leads you to is worth its weight in gold – or tears – if work has been particularly difficult for you.[8] Please don't let the negatives just remain that. See how the Lord can turn them into great things in his service. For example, the lesson David's life teaches us when he had *a really bad day at the office* in 1 Samuel 30:3–6, has been such a blessing to countless other leaders. Faced with life-threatening difficulties on every side, and especially from his men who wanted to stone him because they were overwhelmed with grief, he learned to find his strength in God alone. As any kind of leader, you will need to do that – many times.

EVERYONE LEADS SOMEONE

Please also don't think all this is for the 'really great' leaders of the Bible, history, or contemporary church life, but not for you. It is for us all. God is sovereignly in control of all our lives and has planned for us to be who we are, and will use all these lessons to make us a blessing *as we trust him*.

One of my friends, whom I first met when we were studying geography and playing hockey together, Phil Moon, now leads a thriving church in Brighton. He very kindly encouraged me to write my first book, and then added a comment on the inside. The gist goes like this, 'If God can do this with Ray in Bedford, he can do it with anyone, anywhere.' Another titled his review 'Distinctly Underwhelming'. It was warmly positive, but part of the attraction was 'this is in reach'. I love these comments – God uses 'the ordinary' to achieve his extraordinary. It is worth referring you to Malcolm Gladwell's insightful book, *David & Goliath: Underdogs, Misfits and the Art of Battling Giants* if you are feeling pretty discouraged by a perception that you lack 'what it takes'.[9] It will make you realise that God takes the 'things that are not' to confound the wise and powerful (1 Cor. 1:28) – and is still doing so with you and me today.

You may be a single parent 'leading' your only child, you may lead a spouse, or you together may lead a family with '2.4 children'. You may lead a home group, or a task team, or a ministry in a para-church organisation. You may lead a small, medium, awkward-sized, or large church, or a company or organisation with multiple services, multiple-outlets, or multi-site options.[10] But you will most certainly face *the greatest leadership challenge of all* – leading yourself.[11] We all lead; the question is whether we lead poorly, or well, in the various spheres the Lord entrusts us with. He takes it seriously (see his warning and sense of disappointment in Luke 16:8b–12), and so should we. Part of what will help you become a better leader is to consciously acknowledge God's planning, and reflect upon what he has already made you up to this point in your life. And then recommit yourself to him and see what he may do.

Endless other leadership lessons have been planned by him in your life. It may be from your recreation – playing in a band or orchestra (see the article on how hard it is to play *second fiddle* – as many of us must[12]); or lessons from the sports you're involved in – or avoid! Lessons may come from your pocket-money jobs. For me, some came from a (very) early morning paper round, and from fruit-picking in the warm endless summers of youth. They may come from your holidays, or your interests – even from stamp collecting for all I know.

FROM YOUR EARLIEST YEARS

They will most certainly come from your family experiences, *whatever* they have been. It is said that 90 per cent of all we know, we learn before we are five. Be that as it may, and whatever the balance between nature and nurture, family life can prepare us for servant-leadership. Yes, most definitely the negatives of genetic inheritance or the horrendous sorrows some experience in family life can cause long-term problems. Some will need special help to deal with the worst of this.[13]

The Johari Window*

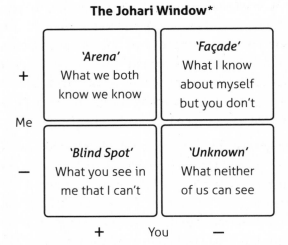

+ Me	**'Arena'** What we both know we know	**'Façade'** What I know about myself but you don't
—	**'Blind Spot'** What you see in me that I can't	**'Unknown'** What neither of us can see

+   You   **—**

* Adapted. Named after its originators, Joseph Luft and Harrington Ingham. The aim of conversation and mutual listening is to increase the area of the upper left quadrant. It takes honesty and humility; characteristics well worth cultivating by God's grace.

All of us can profit from a reflection on the Johari diagram. Ask a friend or a spouse to work this through with you. It is useful in everyone's case, but especially important for the long-term effectiveness of a leader, if it is addressed now. Blind spots that are left that way can be especially damaging (see Jesus' words in Matthew 23).

Don't despise the obvious: for many, 'I know my Mum (and Dad) loves me' is a great reality. To be loved securely and consistently *is a great plus*. As an adult, to replicate that love and direct it to others is a key leadership issue. Too often churches, despite the rhetoric, feel like loveless places. Is this because leaders who set the tone haven't reflected on family, and then Divine, love enough?[14] Or maybe they got shipped off to boarding school, or had largely absent working parents at too young an age for love to have been felt and become ingrained?

Family love, one of the great blessings of God's 'common grace to all' is also a place where we learn 'tough love'. Family love is no good if we are spoilt rotten. At its best, it is love that trains us for the real world. Being made to do chores may be because Dad is lazy, but it may be because our parents want us to be a kind spouse when we were older, and this is one way to get us out of our selfish conceitedness (Heb. 12:7–11).

Receiving encouragement in all its forms, especially when coming from a 'significant other' such as a parent, will remind us how important this is when we lead others.[15] And your earliest memories of family happiness will help you remember that you now belong to the most wonderful family of all, and that your Father has the greatest joy, beyond all imagination, awaiting all his children in his new heavens and new earth. This will spur you on when life and leadership get tough (Heb. 12:1–3).

So take time to reflect on all of this. Perhaps even take the trouble to write something down about your most significant family memories, and the habits and characteristics that God has formed in you.

SPIRITUAL CHARACTER FORMATION IS KEY

Now you may be asking, why go through all of this in a booklet about Christian leadership? Why not just get on with it? Remember Donald Macleod's comment earlier. Without starting where God started – when you were born, then when you were 'born again', you may just miss the obvious. It isn't just about being appointed officially as a 'leader'. God is at work and will use you *as you trust him*. And trusting him is a key leadership issue.

I come from Bedford. Our town's most famous son is John Bunyan. He was a greatly gifted preacher. Odds on you would have never heard of him, unless he had learned to trust God when it seemed like life was out of his control. In his prime as a man and as a leader, he was arrested for preaching the gospel, and imprisoned in the town for 12 long years. It looked like a disaster at every level. But Bunyan embraced God's overruling and trusted him. That's why you have heard of the tinker from Bedford. For in prison he wrote *The Pilgrim's Progress*. Never out of print, translated into endless languages, helpful to countless millions. Without prison he would have been the leader of a small town church. Absolutely fine. But God specialises in taking the weak things, and the small people, and multiplying beyond counting. Bunyan couldn't have imagined what God would do – he had to live life going into an unknown future. He had to live by faith – just as you and I do. So put yourself at God's disposal and leave the results with him.

Before we get onto more of the nuts and bolts of church leadership, what else should we be looking to develop in terms of general characteristics? Paul Mallard recently summed it up like this – 'Bible reading and prayer, then Bible reading and prayer'.[16]

Over his long Christian life and experience as a pastor, he has noted how often this issue of personal Bible reading and consistent prayer undergirds a fruitful life, whatever service God gives us. He is not alone in thinking this. A massive survey of Christian believers in the USA, entitled 'Reveal', found that virtually all those who had progressed to become 'mature' (as measured by a variety of indicators), had this practice as a bedrock to their lives.[17]

I am not saying it is easy. Tim Keller, in his recent book *Prayer* admitted how weak he was in this for far too long. It was when he was diagnosed with cancer and when his wife, Kathy, challenged him that he began to develop a more consistent, intimate and joyful personal prayer life, and a deepening relationship with the Saviour. She asked him that if he knew that he had to take a pill every day or he would die the next, what would he do? In the light of his cancer experience his response was, 'I'd make sure I took it every day!' 'So treat prayer like that pill!' was her retort. He has, and we all have been even more blessed through his ministry because of it.[18] So that preparation is worth getting grounded in, whatever stage you are in the leadership issue.

SOME HINTS AND TIPS ABOUT TRAINING

Some will have realised that God is already leading into what is called 'The Pastoral Ministry'; that is, church leadership involving teaching God's people his Word and taking care of his 'flock' (Acts 20:28). To be better prepared you may have already embarked on, or are considering, some kind of training course. There are very many available. They can be invaluable to future usefulness.

Some involve a thorough intellectual preparation. Make the most of this if you can avail yourself of the opportunity. *Furnishing the mind is vital.* I had only been a Christian for a couple of months when the great Dr Martyn Lloyd-Jones was the guest speaker at our church anniversary in the little Fenland town of Warboys. Being informed that there were many young people attending, he changed his sermon and spoke powerfully from Daniel chapter 1 on the importance of doing this very thing, to the capacity God has given us. I have never forgotten his preaching. We are all different, so comparisons are odious and unnecessary; it is about being who we are and using the gifts God has entrusted to us. Do what you can to get good intellectual and doctrinal training.

Many will learn alongside others, so form a 'band of brothers' which will stand you in good stead in years to come. Throughout your life, keep encouraging one another, whichever 'open door' God gives each person (1 Cor. 16:9; see also Rom.16:3–15).

All should try to find an already established leader to provide some kind of mentoring training. It is the one thread that seems to run through the preparation of God's leaders in the Bible. Moses and Joshua, Elijah and Elisha, Paul and Timothy (and others; 2 Tim. 2:2), and above all, the Lord Jesus with the Twelve, all point to how crucial this is. Whatever training scheme you may follow, *don't neglect this aspect*.

Good leaders will want to help here. Remember how Paul, even after the confusing and emotionally draining difference of judgement with Barnabas over John Mark (Acts 15:36–40), didn't shy away from this, but immediately began to invest in another young man, Timothy, and develop him as a leader (Acts 16:1–5). The Pastoral Epistles evidence how the relationship was long-lasting and how confident Paul was that Timothy could be a 'man of God ... thoroughly equipped for every good work' (2 Tim. 3:17, NIV 1984) because of the way God's Word had provided for him – and us (2 Tim. 3:16).

All of this *takes time* so do not worry about rushing it. I am about to tell you how long it took me before I felt I got anywhere. I may have been a slow learner (!) but probably I am fairly typical.

But let's now move onto some of the matters that affect leadership in a local church. What should you be thinking about that?

LOCAL CHURCH LEADERSHIP

All organisations face the Why?, Who?, What?, When?, and How? questions of leadership. A wide variety of responses are given. For Christians, seeking to be faithful to the Lord Jesus, and in obedience to his commands, the Bible is determinative of their answers. Even so, a wide variety of answers can still be given!

Church leadership in the Independent Free Churches is an attempt to work out in practice an approach to both church and leadership that is consciously grounded in positive biblical teaching. Its first concern is to be faithful to all the Lord, through his apostles, says he wants for his church. It believes that a sufficient Scripture has enough clear teaching, wisdom, and guidance for the church not to 'have to make it all up as it goes along'.[19]

So the answer to the 'Why?' of leadership? Because Jesus says he wants leaders for his church, and he provides them. 'It was he who gave some to be ... pastors and teachers.' (Eph. 4:11, NIV 1984). He also tells us who the 'Who?' should be, by laying down clear 'recognition criteria' so that the church members could identify them. So passages such as 1 Timothy 3:1–7 and Titus 1:5–9 clearly help point out this answer (note that the church doesn't *make* leaders, it *recognises* the ones Christ has given).

The 'What?' is more complex as apostolic commands and example show a multifaceted role. But verses such as Ephesians 4:12, 'to prepare God's people for works of service ...' (NIV 1984) show us that leaders primarily are enablers of God's people. They catalyse and release others into action, encouraging them in all spheres of life to please and glorify the Lord. They provide wholesome teaching, they protect from dangers, they watch over and guard (see Jn. 21:15–17; Acts 20:17–35; 2 Tim. 1:13–14). They are to be examples to all, especially in commending the gospel to others who don't yet believe (1 Tim. 4:12b; 2 Tim. 4:1–4).

The 'When?' is partly answered by the criteria – i.e. when those qualities are seen, then recognition can take place. But 'after appropriate training' is part of that answer too, as Apostolic example testifies and as I have already alluded to above (see Acts 15:36 – 16:5; 2 Tim. 3:10–17).

Finally the 'How?' is somewhat contained in the 'Who?'. The criteria are given to the whole church, not just to a select few. Individuals are to judge of their willingness (1 Tim. 3:1), the church of their worthiness. Members and leaders together in consultation identify those Christ has given to them, and then publicly set them apart (see Acts 14:23, Tit. 1:5). Leaders lead this, but members consent (see also Acts 15:22). This will help you a great deal as you seek the Lord's guidance for your own service.

How are others responding to your service in Word and Deed? What do they react positively to? What honest feedback do you get? It is a tremendous help to have God's people confirm what gifts he has given you and direct you to which avenues for service in the church may be most appropriate. It is not a 'Lone Ranger' thing.

Clearly all these answers can be fleshed out at great length. But the point is that church leadership should be patterned on the Word of its King, Lord and Saviour, never forgetting that the church belongs to him, for it was 'bought with his own blood' (Acts 20:28).

So how does all this fit in with what you are exploring?

Being involved as a Christian believer in a church which is committed to obeying Christ's Word is key. Great if you already belong to such a church, find one if you aren't.

Two great issues then arise which will help you make a way forward. First, you must judge of your willingness to serve. It is not a competition or a reward, but God gives leaders a desire to serve people by leading them in God's ways (see 1 Tim. 3:1; 1 Pet. 5:2–3). This will feel like a mixture of burden on the heart, an eagerness in the spirit, a humility in the soul, and a must-do priority in the will.

Second, your church fellowship (guided by it leaders) must judge two things:

1) Your character

2) Your capability

Let's look at these. Leaders are not perfect – you know that already. But local church leadership is about a degree of Christlikeness. The qualifications in the Scriptures don't paint 'spiritual gigantism', but 'maturity' in various areas of life. Most leadership qualifications are to do with this; it is the battleground on which you will be assaulted by the wiles of the devil. That's why it needs testing.

The fellowship will also want to help you estimate your gifting and its relative strength. Their 'voice' on your 'voice' is vital. As you begin to preach, teach, guide, listen, advise, comment, care, and pray in countless small ways, it will help them and you see whether the Lord is equipping you for 'official leadership' (elder, minister, pastor, vicar and the other synonymous terms), or perhaps 'unofficial' leadership (e.g. home group leader, task team leader).

Their views and your gifting may develop over time. Notice how two 'deacons' in Acts 6 both became preachers/evangelists later (Stephen in Acts 7 and Philip in chapter 8) It is not necessarily 'fixed' (for example, see how deacons in 1 Timthy 3:10 must be 'tested' first and then be appointed). Some people's gifting will be stronger than others (see 1 Timothy 5:17 which gives criteria for which leaders should be financially supported when money is tight). Some may have gifting strong enough for a church to ask that person to go into training and then into 'whole-time' paid leadership, while others serve as leaders without necessarily being paid.

When your willingness combines to the church's positive judgement on your suitability of character and gifting, you can be assured of God's 'call' into leadership. That process all might take time, but don't rush it as it serves as a vital check on ensuring the church is led well, and that you are in the place God wants you to be.

But let me tell you a bit more of how that developed in my life as serving opportunities opened up.

AN ARTICLE THAT DESCRIBED ME

I was intrigued. An article described 'the career path' of a Christian minister, but it was so different from what I was expecting.[20] Rather than 'a sense of calling', theological training at a college, service in various churches, and a retirement spent in committees, he described four very different stages of his personal development. As I read on, that ominous sense of something missing in my life increased, and I suspected it might be missing in other Christian leaders' lives. What was it?

He described starting out as a 'preacher boy' in his 20s, full of energy and enthusiasm, lacking in capability, but keen to improve. That sounded familiar as I recalled my own early efforts to communicate God's Word.

Then came 'the pastor' period. He realised that there was a lack of depth in his preaching, a missing connection to people in all the complexity of their lives, and a superficiality about helping them with their problems. So he had tried to gain experience and a more mature approach to people with difficulties. I resonated with that as I too had tried in my early 30s to more effectively understand and guide people.

I suspect that's where many ministers arrive, and perhaps stay. 'Pastor-teachers', the fully finished article. Able to handle God's Word correctly, and able to guide people well. The gospel minister surely is now formed?

Except the article didn't stop there. Another two stages were to come. What had he gone through that I didn't even know was yet ahead of me, and which you may underplay too?

His third developmental area was his growth as a church 'leader'. By this he didn't mean 'boss', 'biggest ego' or 'Mr Power-broker', but the shouldering of a certain kind of responsibility that enabled the church to go forward more positively in accomplishing its God-given mission. There were two aspects to this. First, was a mature Christian character. I hoped something of that was there in my life, although it is sad to see how many ministries are soured if not ruined by character flaws such as being over-controlling, touchiness over criticism, and fear of change.

The second was the acquisition of necessary leadership skills. Here I was in trouble. For despite all the formational life experiences I have described above, my theological background (Reformed, Independent Free Church, Baptist), for all its strengths, tended towards a narrative of suspicion about the words 'leadership' and 'skills'.

Nevertheless, the article described exactly the kinds of problems in church life I was experiencing. And exactly the problems I observed in evangelical churches all around me. Basic leadership mistakes were accounting far too often for churches losing their sense of gospel priorities. Many of the notorious 'church splits' could be traced to this weakness, rather than to doctrinal aberration or moral compromise.

This led the author to 'skill-up' – reading and learning about leadership matters until he began to imbibe them. He then found that this phase of his life led to strategically important progress for the church he served.

I soon realised that there was a huge hole in my Christian ministry that needed filling. But where to start? A friend pointed me to resources he had found helpful, but which were outside of my normal range of awareness. Books, conferences, men I could talk to about leadership, all began to help me; and the church benefited. But I had a lot of catching up to do all throughout my 40s. So if you are in your earlier years, make the most of consciously learning before I did.

The final stage he described was becoming a 'preacher man', now not only able to expound faithfully, and counsel wisely, but to envision and challenge the church to realise its God-given potential. But also able to lead it into practical ways of translating all that into 'real action on the ground'.

Well, I certainly wasn't there yet, but I could see how some older men I respected had consciously developed in all four of these stages of 'a man of God', exemplifying what the author described. It gave me something to aspire to, and areas of development to work at. Perhaps it might you too. For in all the theological writing and discussion about Christian ministry, *leadership* gets neglected, and churches suffer.

So I now want to move on to explore some more areas of church leadership that might help us all develop mature character, and improve our skill set.

A TALK THAT ENLIGHTENED ME

Five letters became significant to me. They were discovered at a conference that discussed key leadership issues.[21] The first two were 'PC'. Not 'Politically Correct' or 'Parish Church', but 'Prevailing Church'. That is to say, a church going forward to fulfil its God-given redemptive potential, irrespective of its size or cultural setting.

To achieve that, the first element was 'T', standing for 'Teaching'. 'PC' is shaped by great Bible teaching. Christian ministers want to aim to preach messages that are true, faithful, clear, Spirit-filled, and urgently relevant. Though our gifting will vary, as the Lord decides, we each have to be faithful with the gifting assigned to us. We are told to, '*Do your best* to present yourself to God as one approved, a workman who does not need to be ashamed and who correctly handles the word of truth' (2 Tim. 2:15, emphasis added, NIV 1984). We are to 'fan into flame' the gifts we have (2 Tim. 1:6). This is important, for as our preaching gift strengthens, our congregations will be enabled to grow (or won't be held back). But on its own, great preaching may not grow a prevailing church, but perhaps only a large audience. When the great teacher moves on, retires or dies, the crowd may just disperse.

So another element is 'V' for 'Volunteers': motivated members who serve in the church in a variety of ministries. Sometimes in the past this was an emphasis framed as *over against* preaching. One might hear a comment such as: 'Instead of so much dull preaching we need every-member ministry.' Churches shifted their focus into other, and what were deemed more exciting, gifts. Many churches then went on, sadly, to fragment over power struggles, squabbles over who had what gifts, and arguments about which gifts were for today's church and which were not. Thankfully most have now recovered a better perspective, with Bible teaching releasing and preparing God's people into works of service in the church, the community, and their everyday 'front lines' (Eph. 4:12).

But there was one final comment, one key that enables teaching to more thoroughly impact and empower people to serve. What was that? 'L' for 'Leadership'; captured in a handy and memorable summary:

T + L + V = PC

*Teaching + Leadership + Volunteers
= a Prevailing Church*

Great teaching doesn't automatically release volunteers into service, *leaders enable that*. Leaders take the teaching into their own lives, being formed and shaped by it, then, and most importantly of all, they personally *encourage* others to live it out in various acts of kindness, deeds of service, labours of love and ministries of mercy. Churches need this kind of leadership throughout their life and structure – small-group leaders, ministry team leaders, leaders of homes, as well as the overall church leadership. Any wise church leader should realise that it's a multi-person thing operating at many levels, not just the leader working in isolation. It's no part of Jesus' pattern for his church to have one man alone running everything. Leadership is always a multi-person, variably gifted way forward. 'Elders' is invariably plural in NT church contexts, and even the apostle Paul noted it as an unusual thing when he was alone, and always desired to work alongside others in a team approach (see e.g. Acts 14:23; 1 Thes. 3:1).

All this made me think, and think hard. As a pastor I had become so used to preparing talks, and so taken up with fighting 'pastoral fires' that I hadn't had time to train other leaders. What attempts I had made seemed weak and ineffective, and sometimes I felt guilty if I spent time with capable people while it felt the needy were being neglected.

I realised that I had intentionally to give quality time to training others, but that they didn't all have to be aspiring pastor-teachers. Those who stood out as being willing to *encourage others* were the basic raw material that I should work with. They in turn would act to empower the whole church to serve more effectively.

So, some questions: Have you experienced a plurality of leadership in any shape? Have you sought God's leading about joining a leadership team? If you are already a leader, where do you put your energy and time? Into T, L, or V, or a balance between all three? Are you succeeding in releasing other members to be 'whole-life disciples', as well as serving in the church?

A PASSAGE THAT HELPED ME – *ACTS 6:1–7*

I have written about this at length elsewhere, but I want to underscore some important lessons for Christian leaders from this passage.[22]

First is the connection between 'growth' and 'groans'. I wasn't prepared for this. I had assumed that if our church grew a bit, many problems would diminish or even disappear (well, you can always hope). Growth would equal re-energised believers, new people with something to offer, and a stronger confidence in what the gospel could do. This passage alerted me to the fact that growth may bring unexpected problems. It showed me that all churches of whatever size and relative 'success' have attendant difficulties. All have their 'plus' and 'minus' side, and wise leaders face up to what that might mean for the size and stage their own church is in.

Second was the recognition that though great prayerfulness and faithful teaching are necessary conditions for church health and growth, they aren't always sufficient on their own. The church in Acts 6 needed wise leadership that understood how to implement a 'management solution' to a very threatening and tricky problem. That is, they knew how to problem-solve by *organising* cleverly and effectively. No amount of preaching, or even prayer, would have solved the presenting problem which they faced – hungry widows who spoke a different language from others in the church. They needed skills to properly diagnose and identify what was going wrong, and to problem-solve with an actionable solution.

Third was they had to take the people with them. They brilliantly gained ownership by all (see Acts 6:5), and everyone felt involved. The solution was 'a group thing', not just a diktat. Perhaps this is one of the most difficult areas of leadership, where many feel unprepared and nervous. It is an area which deserves more detailed treatment than possible in this short booklet, but suffice it to say, a belief in the priesthood of all believers and the ministry of the indwelling Holy Spirit in all of his people will encourage leaders not to fear the gaining of ownership by God's people of these key decisions.

Thus they did all of this and the church came through with flying colours (Acts 6:7). The Word was released to greater effectiveness because they dealt with an obstacle to growth.

We don't have to solve the difficulties of neglected Greek-speaking widows now, but what may be the equivalents that leaders need to address? These sorts of problems may be significantly blocking gospel progress today!

All this came as a culture shock to me. After all, as with many other churches, we had our 'proper' biblical structure with duly appointed office-bearers – elders and deacons. We assumed therefore that everything organisationally must all be alright. But we never really approached solving gospel blockages with the approach that Acts 6 taught. Learning to identify what was holding the church back, being proactive with workable solutions, empowering others to make practical differences in church life and so forth were all out of our comfort zones. But what a difference it has made as we grappled with Acts 6, started to lead better, and release the church to have a greater impact. It is well worth realising ahead of time that problems like this may confront you when you come to lead.

If you are already in the early years of being a church leader, you may need to get some time away with other leaders to have a hard look at your own church life, and to ask if there are any obvious things inhibiting gospel progress. You must encourage honest input, for creative tension can be very valuable, but also must focus the leadership team on practicable paths forward. You must also set a strong spiritual temperature of dependency on God, otherwise it all just becomes another 'to-do' list with 'tick box' responses.

So far we have been thinking about some of the skills that you need to lead a church well – wise leadership, working with colleagues, gaining ownership, empowering others, having a vision for gospel effectiveness, and seeing the members impact the community through their daily lives. But how do you acquire these skills? Some help may come from the next section.

A HABIT THAT SHAPED ME

You may have gained the impression that my formal ministry training left me inadequately prepared. That wouldn't be at all fair on those who invested in me. Nor would it reflect a priceless habit that their training established in my life. What was that? The habit of becoming a life-long learner. Leaders don't so much 'get trained' but learn to keep learning.

I had seen this in others. Let me relate an outstanding example. I was in the Evangelical Library in the mid-1970s researching for my PhD on Puritanism and science. There was a huge 600 plus-page tome to tackle, Charles Webster's *The Great Instauration* (even a researcher might avoid a book with a title like that!). Only one person had already borrowed it from the library, and his name was inside on the borrower's list. You guessed it – Dr Lloyd-Jones, and that in his late 70s! Life-long learner or what?

So, how do you develop this habit in the midst of a busy life?

First, expose yourself to the best. You can now easily listen to some great contemporary preachers on the Internet. They will have greater gifts no doubt, they will have a different style, they will be outwardly more blessed, but you can learn a lot from them (yet don't ape their every inflection!).

Choose to read the best – the best of the past and the best of the present. You can't read even a fraction of all that is produced, so get good advice on what really counts. We all have our favourite authors, issues, periods in history and doctrinal emphases, and that is fine. But get out of your comfort zone too. Read deep *and wide*. Another example of what I mean comes from the life of Phillip E. Johnson, author of *Darwin on Trial*. He was a law lecturer at Berkeley. While on sabbatical in London, he noticed a couple of books in a shop window that caught his interest. As a piece of 'light reading' different from his normal legal fare, he worked his way through them. One put a case for Darwinism, the other questioned it. He was so struck by the poor arguments employed by the proponent that he delved deeper, and a series of highly influential books was the result of reading outside his normal range.

You can also get alongside good leaders via their blogs, email, phone or by asking to meet up. Get to conferences where great ministry and great leadership are exemplified and discussed. You won't always agree with all you see and hear, so filter out what is not wise or even right, and then refine what is good and helpful.

Talk with peers honestly about the plus and minus matters you face. Ask if they face similar problems too, or others you aren't aware of, and ask how they may have overcome the difficulties. No solutions can be exactly the same, but their wise insights may help you. Ministers' fraternals could help more than they sometimes do, and we need to so shape them that they become unmissable. We all learn best from fellow practitioners rather than from external experts or internal critics, so it is vital to develop healthy accountability relationships.

Second, some kind of feedback group may help immensely. A small team to help appraise what you do is useful. It may be a weekly group looking at Sunday services; what went well, what could go better next time. If this is a regular feature rather than just occasional, the lessons will be reinforced and improvements will be more noticeable. It is helpful if all the members of a feedback group take part in being appraised so that everyone knows how it feels to receive constructive criticism.

A coach or mentor has a slightly different role. A coach's job is to observe carefully and advise accordingly, even though they may not be as capable as the person they are helping. Someone you trust, who you know has your best interests at heart, may be able to say some difficult-to-hear but necessary truths to help you improve. Such a person may be able to point to resources to use, habits to develop, or weaknesses to work on. How you lead worship meetings and members' meetings, how you preach, counsel and lead other leaders may all benefit from wise coaching. An 'every now and then' exposure to a coach can lead to steady progress.

Can you find time for all of this? Not in an ordinary week. But if you block some time for them, they become more doable, and soon you will discover that you can't do without them.

AN OBSERVATION THAT STARTLED ME

I mentioned earlier the 'awkward-sized' church (notice the word 'sized', it's more than just 'awkward'). I hadn't noticed it, but we certainly felt its effects. It was eye-opening to come across literature about numbers and organisational complexity and realise that we were experiencing the confusion that can arise from this.

Growth from a small church into a larger size brought to a head a decision-making challenge that many leaders will face. It is this: 'Do we church-plant or do we seek to grow numerically bigger where we are?' I realise that some reading this may feel that they'd love to be in the situation where either of those options was a realistic one, but just at the moment they feel they are battling to survive.

There is no 'one size fits all' solution. But whatever route you take, a leader must keep painting a *gospel-driven vision*. Too often church problems preoccupy us, negativity about seeing conversions becomes endemic, and poor evangelistic methodology leaves us ineffective. Good leadership must keep addressing the hearts and minds of Christians with this, so that when decisions are to be made, the underlying motivation will be shaped by *gospel considerations* more than personal taste, preference and convenience.

When a 'gospel culture' is established, then attention will have to be given to issues such as team development, staff appointments, financial provision, geographical location of facilities, training and so forth. Leadership teams will need to pay careful attention to a variety of these issues, yet in the end will also have to step out in adventurous faith.

I had often ducked all of this. I was busy enough with preaching and pastoring. Aren't matters like this only for the experienced, highly capable and successful? But I have found it's like having children. You never will feel as if you are ready, you learn along the way, but then feel out of your depth as the next stage of their growing lives soon comes round! So with church leadership, you don't have to be an expert before you lead the church forward.

It helps to talk to other leaders who have faced these issues. For example, they may have great insights into how to better run the church's finances, they may know people looking for an appointment as an assistant pastor or youth worker and connect you to them, and they may point you to resources that could develop better teamwork. It is important for more experienced leaders to give time to help younger men in this way. Biblically we all may be 'bishops' ('episkopos' is used of all elders in the NT), but some must assist and advise their fellow-labourers in the gospel, even if that arrangement is more tacit than formal.

THE CHALLENGES THAT STILL FACE ME

Finally, the future! What will you at the beginning, and I towards the end of active service, still face as Christian leaders? First is the 'church-life curve'. As has been pointed out many times, the famous 'bell-shaped curve' may describe the beginning, the middle and the death of living, organised, things. The local church may be one such example of this. (See Gary McIntosh, *Taking Your Church to the Next Level* for exceptionally helpful insights. Don't be put off by the title!)[23]

We need to have an honest look: have we plateaued after some growth? Are we declining, despite a lot of hard work? Are we seeing some recovery after a period of stagnation, with new people and some fresh gospel vision? Such roller coaster curves can be pretty scary (if you are a pessimist by nature), or exhilarating (if not). Leaders constantly need to bring gospel initiatives to help the church keep growing out of stagnation or a declining tendency. These are never easy, and they will demand faith, prayerfulness and courage. You will need to identify and bring on other leaders, raise money and take risks. Without hubris, presumption on God, or browbeating the people of God, leaders need to keep the church missional.

All of us will need some of that attitude that the Cornishman Billy Bray exemplified: 'If they were to put me in a barrel, I would shout glory out through the bunghole!'

Second come the challenges of the 'personal-growth curve'. This should be the classic 'S' curve which has a steady upward trend (despite the 'blips' now and then). Am I willing to keep growing as a Christian *disciple*, not just as a minister? Will I be willing to serve the Lord even as I, in time, lay down direct leadership responsibilities? Too many of us invest our significance in the work we do. Take away our relatively high-profile 'up there at the front' and we may flounder. We mustn't serve to feed a hungry ego's need for achievement, admiration, recognition, gratitude or self-expression. Without an increasing depth to my own personal spirituality, an increasing capability in public leadership functionality may be the last thing the church needs!

Third, and finally, comes that challenge of passing on the baton. The handovers in relays are always fraught with tension. Leadership handover is no different. It seems weird to say this to potential new leaders, but never leave this until it is too late.

Often at this point, as we survey the church and our work, we can end up being disappointed with it, ourselves, and even God. Pour contempt on all of this. Don't judge the Lord by feeble sense, to paraphrase the great hymn-writer William Cowper.

I think the apostle Paul points to a better way: leaders *intentionally plan* to pass on the baton. Paul, towards the end of his life, surveyed four generations – himself, Timothy, 'reliable men', and 'others' (see 2 Tim. 2:2, NIV 1984). He made provision in his priorities and planning to ensure, as much as he could, that this would happen. We must too. This may involve raising extra funds to train men, sharing more of the preaching to give younger men supervised experience, and more honest discussion about key leadership issues.

CONCLUSION

Left to ourselves and faced with all of this, who would not cry, '... who is equal to such a task?' (2 Cor. 2:16, NIV 1984). But an ever-gracious Lord, who delights to help us in our weakness, is near to all those who call on his name. His resources can enable us to face all these leadership challenges. I am convinced of that, our forefathers proved that, and above all, his Word declares it.

TEN TIPS

Let me conclude by highlighting some leadership lessons, albeit simplistically, in a short list.

1. Privilege

Being called by the Lord and set apart by his people for leadership is a huge privilege. We should honour that by making the most of the opportunities that we are given, whatever our place in ministry.

2. Patience

God grows leaders, but growth takes time. Remember that none of your life's various experiences need be wasted, but if you are willing to learn, they can all be turned to greater leadership fruitfulness.[24]

3. Character

God blesses great likeness to Christ more than great giftedness. This world doesn't see it like that, but churches with holy pastors are blessed places. So 'guard your heart' (Prov. 4:23), and 'Watch your life and doctrine closely' (1 Tim. 4:16). Character really does count when it comes to leadership.

4. Connection

Learn to be a good listener. Tim Keller urges young preachers to spend far more time listening to people. It will help you preach better because you will connect to their lives, but it will also gain their affection. They may admire your gifts if you preach well, but they will love you as a leader if you share life with them.[25] It is easier to trust and follow a leader you love, rather than just respect.

5. Team

People may laud the rugged individualist's achievements, but effective leadership is always more about harnessing the synergy of teams of people. When teams work well, God is glorified, much is accomplished, and participants experience fulfilment. Remember the acronym TEAM = 'Together Everyone Achieves More', and the saying, 'If you want to go fast, go alone. If you want to go far, go together.' So learn all you can about great teamwork, and how you can help create that.[26]

6. Authority

You need to recall two things: you are a *servant* leader. If you have any tendency towards a controlling behaviour pattern, remember you are a *servant* of the Lord, and a *servant* to his people (1 Pet. 5:1–3). You are there to obey the One, and lovingly support the other. But you also need to remember that you are a servant *leader*. If you don't lead, someone else (less qualified), will step into the vacuum. So you mustn't be afraid of hard calls, difficult decisions, awkward conversations and decisive moments. You have been commissioned by the King for these (see Tit. 1:5,11). Independency enables these two apparent conflicting demands to be met well, and modelled in an attractive way. Make sure it is.

7. Energy

Church leadership is hard work (see Col. 1:28 – 2:1). It involves struggle, sacrifice, and tears (Acts 20:19). Don't resent that. Give it your all. But also recall the poem, 'Elsewhere Perhaps':

The soil is softer,
The tasks less stubborn,
The laughter quicker,
The hearts less worn,
The grass greener...
Elsewhere perhaps.

But the grass is not greener
Elsewhere perhaps.
The grass grows greener
Where you water it.
Now, on this day,
Here, on this task,
On these hearts and mine,
Let the heavens open
And your reign shine.[27]

8. Train

In a relay race the key is to *pass on the baton*. Start investing in other leaders today. Don't wait for a superstar; trust God that he has given you people you can nurture now. A well-trained believer can be a powerful force for good, whatever their gifting.

9. Skills

To carry out your multifaceted responsibilities you will also need to be keenly aware of using limited time well. This is a key leadership skill. Alongside that, you will need to know how to prioritise. Stimulating gospel initiatives, spending time with new/fringe people, and investing in your leadership team have to be right up there if you are to take the church forward. Above all, learn how to encourage people so that they follow you, as you follow Christ.

10. Church

'The local church is the hope of the world' is a well-known leadership saying. The well-led gospel church is God's chosen instrument for fulfilling his redemptive plans for this world. 'Independency' in church government allows churches and leaders to flourish, as there are so many gospel freedoms and opportunities it opens up. It's a joy to be at the centre of that.

But it is a greater and a tremendous joy to recall that the church, including the church where you serve in the future or even now, is Jesus' Bride. You are helping prepare her for a fabulous day! When you hand her over, won't that be something (see 2 Cor. 11:2)? It makes all the effort more than worthwhile.

NOTES

1. Prime, D., *A Christian's Guide to Leadership* (EP, 2005), p. 85.
2. Lewis, C.S., *The Screwtape Letters* (Geoffrey Bles, 1942), pp. 142,143. See also Jesus' words in Matthew 13:22.
3. Warren, R., *The Purpose Driven Church* (Zondervan, 1995), pp. 369–375.
4. British Evangelical Council Study Conference, High Leigh, Hoddesdon, 1993.
5. Hybels, B., *Leadership Axioms* (Zondervan, 2008), pp. 139–141.
6. Kipling, R., 'If' (Accessed at www.poetryfoundation.org/poem/175772, 22 July 2015.)
7. Evans, R., *Ready, Steady, Grow* (IVP, 2014), pp. 48,49, for details of research on just how influential church leaders are in determining the health and progress of church life.
8. Mark Greene and his colleagues' work in this area at the London Institute for Contemporary Christianity have provided an invaluable antidote to too-narrow a focus. See Greene, M., *Fruitfulness on the Frontline* (IVP, 2014); Hudson, N., *Imagine Church* (IVP, 2012).
9. Gladwell, M., *David & Goliath: Underdogs, Misfits and the Art of Battling Giants* (Penguin, 2013).
10. Evans, R., op cit, pp. 17–43.
11. Hybels, B., 'The Leader's Edge' (Willow Creek Association UK, 'Building Life-changing Churches' Conference, April 2002.) Also see Maxwell, J., *The 360° Leader* (Nelson, 2005), especially the section on 'Leading Up', pp. 84–157.
12. Anon, 'Play Second Fiddle' (Accessed at www.threadsuk.com/play-second-fiddle, 22 July 2015.)
13. Davies, G., *Genius, Grief and Grace* (Christian Focus, 2008) for examples of well-known Christians who would have benefited from help, but whom God nevertheless mightily used.
14. Hybels, B., *Leadership Axioms* (Zondervan, 2008), 'Speed of the Leader, Speed of the Team', pp. 94,95.
15. Evans, R., op cit, p. 214.

16. Paul Mallard 'Closing Sermon' (FIEC 'Hub Conference', Newport Pagnell, 18 January 2015).

17. Hawkins, G.L. and Parkinson, C., *Reveal* (Willow Creek Resources, 2007).

18. Keller, T., *Prayer: Experiencing Awe and Intimacy with God* (Hodder & Stoughton, 2014), pp. 9,10.

19. See the important discussion by James Bannerman on this in Evans, R., op cit, pp. 51,52.

20. Despite my best efforts, I haven't been able to trace this particular article.

21. Hybels, B., 'The Leader's Edge' (Willow Creek Association UK 'Building Life-changing Churches' conference, April 2002).

22. Evans, R. op cit, pp. 61–81.

23. McIntosh, G.L., *Taking Your Church to the Next Level* (Baker, 2009).

24. Newton, J., *Letters of John Newton* (BoT, 1965), pp. 13–18, 'Grace in the Blade'.

25. Keller, T., 'The Country Parson' (12/01/2009. http://repc. com/blog/view.jsp?Blog_param=78). See also 'Preaching to the Heart', Occasional paper given at Oak Hill Theological College, 19/11/2008.

26. See, for example, Lencioni, P., *The Five Dysfunctions of a Team* (Jossey-Bass, 2002).

27. 'Elsewhere Perhaps' (London Institute for Contemporary Christianity, Occasional postcard, 2013). Quoted by permission of the author, Mark Greene.

FURTHER READING

The Church of Christ Bannerman, J.
(Banner of Truth, 1960)

Ready, Steady, Grow Evans, R. (IVP, 2014)

Leadership Axioms Hybels, B. (Zondervan, 2008)

Courageous Leadership Hybels, B. (Zondervan, 2002)

Center Church Keller, T. (Zondervan, 2012)

The Five Dysfunctions of a Team Lencioni, P.
(Jossey-Bass, 2002)

The 360° Leader Maxwell, J. (Nelson, 2005)

Staff Your Church for Growth McIntosh, G.
(Baker, 2000)

Taking Your Church to the Next Level McIntosh, G.
(Baker, 2009)

A Christian's Guide to Leadership Prime, D. (EP, 2005)

Relational Leadership Wright, W. (Paternoster, 2000)

MORE IN THIS SERIES

ON BEING A SERVANT OF GOD
Warren Wiersbe
978-1-910587-10-2

THE CALL
Paul Mallard & Trevor Archer
978-1-910587-50-8

WHY FREE CHURCH MINISTRY?
Graham Beynon
978-1-910587-49-2

TO FLY TO SERVE
Adrian Reynolds
978-1-910587-60-7

10Publishing is the publishing house of 10ofThose.
It is committed to producing quality Christian
resources that are biblical and accessible.

www.10ofthose.com is our online retail arm selling
thousands of quality books at discounted prices.

For information contact: **sales@10ofthose.com**
or check out our website: **www.10ofthose.com**